crochet your own
spooky skull garland

Kati Gálusz

becker&mayer! books

Brimming with creative inspiration, how-to projects, and useful information to enrich your everyday life, Quarto Knows is a favorite destination for those pursuing their interests and passions. Visit our site and dig deeper with our books into your area of interest: Quarto Creates, Quarto Cooks, Quarto Homes, Quarto Lives, Quarto Drives, Quarto Explores, Quarto Gifts, or Quarto Kids.

This book is part of the *Crochet in a Day: Crochet Your Own Spooky Skull Garland* kit and is not to be sold separately.

becker&mayer! books titles are also available at discount for retail, wholesale, promotional, and bulk purchase. For details, contact the Special Sales Manager by email at specialsales@quarto.com or by mail at The Quarto Group, Attn: Special Sales Manager, 100 Cummings Center Suite 265D, Beverly, MA 01915 USA.

21 22 23 24 25   5 4 3 2 1

ISBN: 978-0-7603-6943-2

Library of Congress Cataloging-in-Publication Data available upon request.

Author: Katalin Gálusz
Photography: Chris Burrows

Printed, manufactured, and assembled in Shenzhen, China, 05/21.

Distributed by:
Quarto UK, The Old Brewery
6 Blundell Street, London N7 9BH, UK
Allen & Unwin
30 Centre Rd, Scoresby VIC 3179, AUS

Image credits: All stock photographs and design elements © Shutterstock

#340106

Contents

About This Kit

This kit contains the tools and materials you will need to make a 4' (1.25m) garland with four skulls: yarn in white and black; a G/6 (4mm) crochet hook; and a yarn needle.

How to Read the Instructions

Every line starts with the round/row number in bold, and ends with the stitch count in parentheses.

Instructions in square brackets must be repeated the specified number of times before continuing with the remaining instructions of the round or row (if any).

Abbreviation Chart

CH	CHAIN OR CHAINS
INC	INCREASE
RND	ROUND
SC	SINGLE CROCHET (US) DOUBLE CROCHET (UK)
SL ST	SLIP STITCH
ST	STITCH OR STITCHES
YO	YARN OVER

Notes on Tools and Materials

YARN

The garland in this book was designed with worsted weight yarn, but you could use any yarn thickness; as long as you choose a matching hook size, your project will turn out just as fine, it will only make the skulls smaller or bigger than the original. You could even use this to create a garland with several differently sized skulls!

HOOK SIZE AND GAUGE

Exact gauge is not important in this project, as long as you work tight enough to create a sturdy fabric that doesn't visibly gape. To achieve this, you will need a hook size smaller than recommended on the yarn's label. The sample garland was crocheted with G/6 (4mm) hook, but this is only a guideline; feel free to experiment to find what best suits your crocheting style.

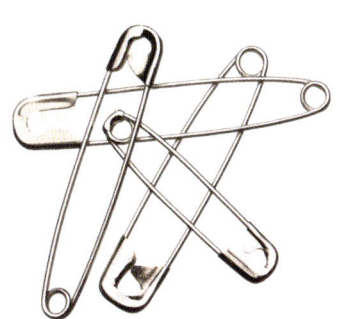

STITCH MARKER

Because most of the project is worked in a continuous spiral without joining, you will need a stitch marker to keep track of your rounds. There are special split-ring markers for crochet, but safety pins or paper clips work just as well.

NEEDLES AND PINS

Blunt tapestry needles are usually recommended for sewing knit and crochet pieces, but for decorative pieces I prefer a chenille needle (or the pointed yarn needle included in this kit), because its sharper point can pierce through yarn if necessary.

Craft pins are necessary to hold pieces in place while you sew them together.

Crochet Stitches and Techniques

This chapter contains a short primer on the techniques you will need to create the garland. If you are new to crochet, I suggest to practice the basics before starting the actual project. Many yarn shops offer classes, or you can look up video tutorials online.

SLIPKNOT

Use this to begin a chain. Make a loop on your yarn a few inches from the end. *(Fig. A)* Insert your hook through the loop and grab the yarn end connected to the skein. Pull the strand through the loop, then tighten the knot. *(Fig. B)*

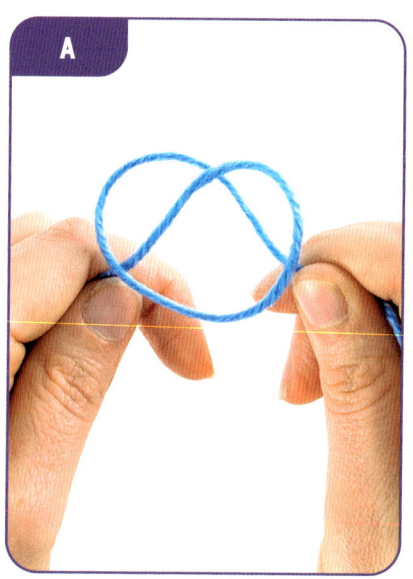

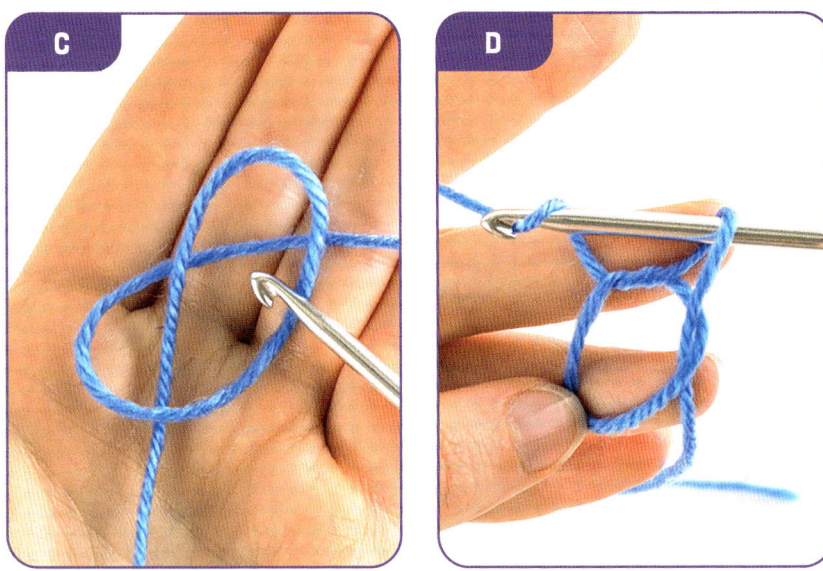

YARN OVER (YO)

Wrap the yarn around your hook from back to front.

MAGIC RING

The magic ring is a nice technique to start working in the round, because it will create a small circle of stitches with no gap in the center.

Make a circle of the yarn. Insert your hook through this ring *(Fig. C)*, YO and draw up a loop *(Fig. D)*, then ch 1. Work the first round of stitches over both the ring and the free yarn end, then pull on the free end to close the ring.

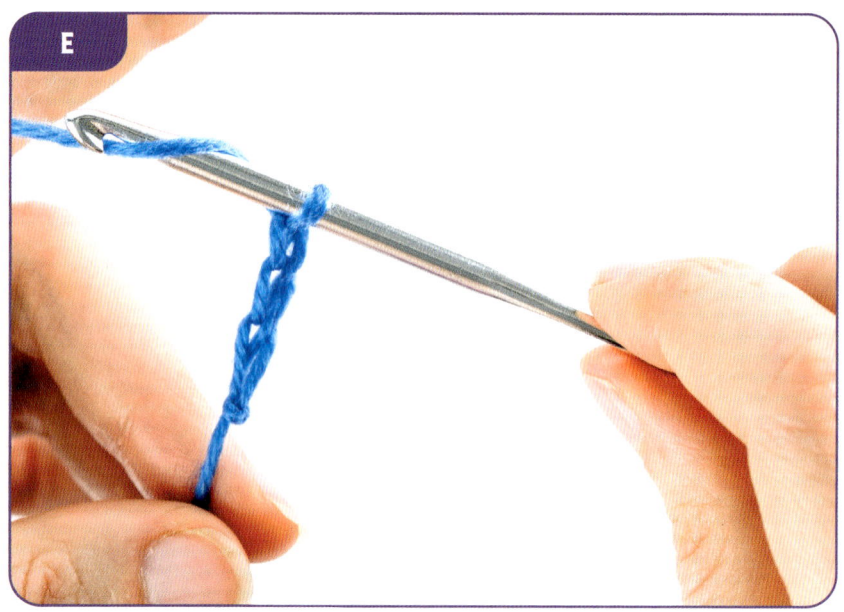

CHAIN (CH)

Make a slipknot first, unless you are in the middle of a piece and already have a loop on your hook. YO, and pull yarn through the loop on hook. Repeat as many times as required. *(Fig. E)*

The loop on the hook doesn't count as chain, so omit it if you are checking the stitch count.

WORKING INTO STITCHES

Every stitch has two strands in a small V shape on top. Insert your hook under both sides of the V unless otherwise specified.

WORKING INTO A CHAIN

Usually, you have to skip the ch nearest to the hook and work your first st in the 2nd or 3rd ch from hook (the pattern will always specify this).

When you look at a row of chains, the front side will look like a series of tiny Vs, and the back will have a single ridge of loops. For the neatest look, insert your hook into the back ridge rather than the front V. *(Fig. F)*

SKIP STITCHES

Leave the required number of st unworked and continue in the next st, working in the same direction as before.

SINGLE CROCHET (SC)

Insert your hook into the st or ch, YO and draw up a loop (pull yarn through st or ch). You will have 2 loops on your hook. YO and pull yarn through both loops on hook. *(Fig. G)*

SLIP STITCH (SL ST)

Insert your hook into the st or ch, YO and pull yarn through both the st or ch and the loop on hook.

INCREASE (INC)

In this pattern, inc always means single-crochet increase: work 2 sc in the same st. *(Fig. H)*

RIGHT & WRONG SIDE

If you are working in rounds without turning, there will be a right and a wrong side. The right side is the side facing you while you work. On the right side, individual stitches resemble small Vs. On the wrong side, they are like an upside down V with a horizontal bar on top.

I

J

WORKING IN CONTINUOUS ROUNDS

The skulls are mostly crocheted in rounds, starting with a small circle of stitches and progressing in a continuous spiral without turning or joining. To keep track of the beginning/end of your rounds, attach a stitch marker in the first st of the round. Move the stitch marker up when you begin the next round. *(Fig. I)*

WORKING IN ROWS

Working in rows means turning your piece at the end of every row and work in the opposite direction in the next row. To allow for this, you will have to crochet a "turning chain" at the end of the row.

Turning chains don't count as regular stitches, so omit them if you are checking your stitch count. *(Fig. J)*

FASTEN OFF

To finish your piece, cut the yarn about 3 inches from your hook (or more, if you will need the yarn end for sewing), and pull the end through the last loop on the hook.

WEAVE IN YARN ENDS

To weave in a yarn end, thread it in a large needle. Stitch it through several stitches at the back of the piece, then snip off the rest as close to the crochet fabric as possible. Try to keep yarn ends under the same color stitches, to make sure the color won't seem through to the front side.

Materials

- **90 YARDS (82M) OF WHITE WORSTED WEIGHT YARN DIVIDED INTO TWO SKEINS**
- **30 YARDS (27M) OF BLACK WORSTED WEIGHT YARN**
- **YARN NEEDLE**
- **G/6 (4MM) CROCHET HOOK**

Finished size: 1 yard (0.9m) long garland

Instructions

Start with winding all three skeins of yarn into balls.
The majority of the skulls will be worked in continuous
rounds, except for the chin/teeth part which is added
using a second ball of yarn and worked in rows.

SKULL BASE (MAKE 4)

RND 1: With white yarn, make a magic ring, ch 1, sc 6 into ring, pull ring tight (6). *(Fig. A)*

RND 2: Inc 6 (12)

RND 3: [sc, inc] 6 times (18)

RND 4: [sc, inc, sc] 6 times (24)

RND 5: [inc, sc 3] 6 times (30) *(Fig. B)*

RND 6: [sc 2, inc, sc 2] 6 times (36)

RND 7: [inc, sc 5] 6 times (42)

RND 8: [sc 3, inc, sc 3] 6 times (48)

RND 9: [inc, sc 7] 6 times (54)

Do not fasten off the yarn! You will resume working with it after crocheting the teeth.

Loosen the live loop on your hook *(Fig. C)*, until it is large enough to tie together with the working yarn *(Fig. D)* - this will prevent your work from unraveling.

Use the second white ball to crochet the teeth.

C

D

TEETH, ROW I: Skip the first 22 st of rnd 9. To join the new yarn, insert your hook into the 23rd st, pull up a loop and ch 1. *(Fig. E)* Work a sc into the same st, then sc 9 (10). *(Fig. F)*

TEETH, ROW II: Ch 1, turn. Sc in each st (10).

TEETH, ROW III: Ch 1, turn. Sc in each st (10).

Fasten off this yarn. *(Fig. G)* Then undo the knot on the other yarn, insert your hook back into the live loop left after rnd 9 and tighten it, so you can continue to crochet around. *(Fig. H)*

RND 10: Sc 4, inc, sc 8, inc, sc 8.

Continue working into the side of the teeth rows: sc 3. *(Fig. I)*

Working into the stitches of Teeth Row III, inc *(Fig. J)*, sc 8, inc. Working into the side of the teeth rows, sc 3. *(Fig. K)*

Working around the rest of the skull, sc 8, inc, sc 8, inc, sc 4 (66).

Sl st in the next st and fasten off. Weave in the yarn ends.

NOSE (MAKE 4)

Note: you might omit these and instead use black thread and yarn needle to embroider the nose onto the skull base by making straight stitches in a triangle shape.

ROW 1: With black yarn, make a slip knot. Ch 3. Working into the back ridge of chains, sc in the 3rd ch from hook. *(Fig. L)*

Fasten off leaving a long yarn end.

Sew on the nose so that its tip is 5 rows from the center of the skull's magic ring. *(Fig. M)*

L

EYES (MAKE 8)

RND 1: With black yarn, make a magic ring and sc 5, pull ring tight (5)

RND 2: Inc 5 (10) *(Fig. N)*

RND 3: [inc, sc] 5 times (15)

Sl st in next st and fasten off leaving a long yarn end for sewing. Weave in the other end.

Pin the eyes to the skull base – they should be about 2 rows from the edge of the skull and their lowest point should be level with the tip of the nose. Sew on the eyes. *(Fig. O)*

Optionally, for a winking skull replace one eye with two stitches in a < shape. *(Fig. P)*

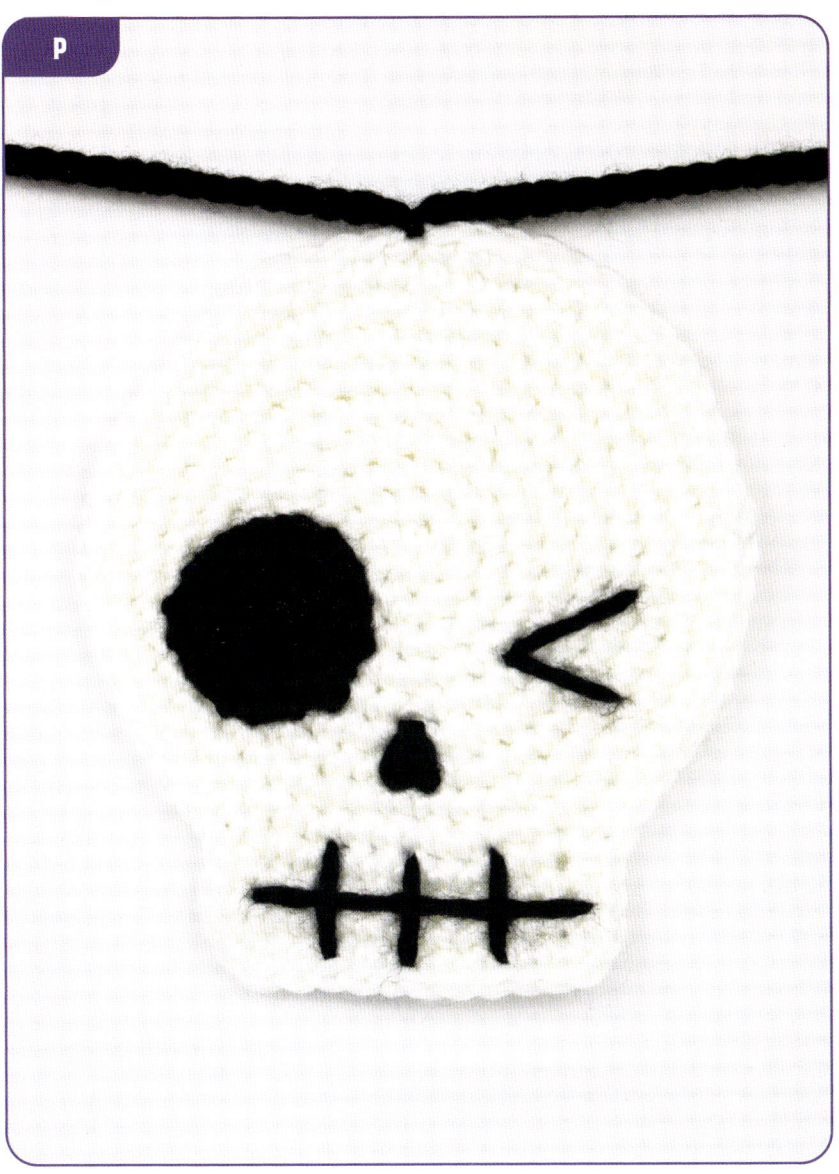

TEETH

To define the teeth, thread a 12" piece of black yarn into the yarn needle. Start with one long horizontal stitch *(Fig. Q)*, then sew 3 vertical stitches evenly distributed. With each of these stitches, pierce the horizontal stitch to anchor it in place *(Fig. R)*. Secure both ends at the backside.

OPTIONAL: BLOCKING

If the skulls won't stay flat, this is a good time to block them. Soak them in water, blot out the excess liquid with a clean towel, then lay them out flat (you can pin them down but it shouldn't be necessary), and let them dry. Alternatively, you can use fabric starch to make sure they won't curl.

CORD

Using black yarn, make a slip knot. Ch 7. Sl st in the 7th ch from hook (this will make a small loop for hanging the garland). *(Fig. S)* Ch until the chain measures 4 1/2". Sl st into the top of the first skull. *(Fig. T)* Continue to ch for 9" *(Fig. U)*, then sl st to the top of the next skull. Repeat 2 more times so that all 4 skulls are attached to the string, then continue to ch for 4 1/2". Finally, ch 7 and sl st to the 7th ch from hook to make the loop for hanging. Fasten off and weave in the yarn ends.

S

Great job! Enjoy your Spooky Skull Garland!

#CrochetInADay

About the Author

KATI GÁLUSZ discovered the world of amigurumi when she wanted to make a unique gift for a toy-collector friend. What started as a quick fling has grown into the love of a lifetime, allowing her to combine her need for creativity with her two main interests, animals and great books and movies. After lavishing her creations on her long-suffering family and friends, she started to sell them on Etsy and share her crochet patterns on Ravelry. When she is not crocheting, she can be usually found with a book in her hand, surrounded by her dogs in her home near Budapest, Hungary.

ALSO
AVAILABLE

crochet your own
reindeer ornaments

crochet your own
**merry and bright
baubles**

crochet your own
**candy cane
ornaments**

Includes
Materials to Make
4 Ornaments

crochet your own
holly jolly garland

crochet your own
festive pumpkin